A Raven Named Grip

HOW A BIRD INSPIRED TWO FAMOUS WRITERS, CHARLES DICKENS AND EDGAR ALLAN POE

Marilyn Singer ✳ illustrated by Edwin Fotheringham

DIAL BOOKS FOR YOUNG READERS

An imprint of Penguin Random House LLC • New York

First published in the United States of America by Dial Books for Young Readers,
an imprint of Penguin Random House LLC, 2021

Text copyright © 2021 Marilyn Singer
Illustrations copyright © 2021 by Edwin Fotheringham

Dial and colophon are registered trademarks of Penguin Random House LLC.
Visit us online at penguinrandomhouse.com.

Library of Congress Cataloging-in-Publication Data is available.

Artwork created on an iPad using Apple Pencil and Procreate app
Design by Jason Henry • Manufactured in China
ISBN 9780593324721 • 10 9 8 7 6 5 4 3 2 1

For Andrew and Sheena

With thanks to the White Memorial Conservation Center
and their fabulous program about ravens.

—M.S.

For my family, as ever

—E.F.

Charley, Katey, and Mamie Dickens were not fond of Grip the raven. The bird chased them around the house. She bit their ankles. She chipped off paint to eat. But the children's father adored the raven. He was Charles Dickens, the most famous writer in all of Great Britain. He'd already published four popular novels, first as installments in magazines and then as books. Even Queen Victoria was a big fan.

In Victorian England, people had many pets besides cats and dogs, especially birds. Today it is illegal to keep wild birds. But back then, people caught or purchased them to keep in cages. Wealthier folks sometimes bought exotic species such as parrots or mynahs. Charles Dickens chose ravens.

In 1841, when he was working on his next book, *Barnaby Rudge*, Dickens decided to make Grip a character in it. The main character was a man who wasn't very clever. But he had a pet raven that was.

Dickens's descriptions of how the bird behaved were accurate and amusing. Ravens can imitate human speech, and Barnaby's raven talked a lot.

Dickens's raven could speak too. Her favorite expression was:

"Halloa, old girl."

It was the last thing she said before she died. The lead paint chips had done her in.

Charles Dickens was very sad. His children were not. During the Victorian era, it was popular to have a pet stuffed when it died, so Dickens sent the raven to a taxidermist. Then he hung Grip in a glass case above his desk to keep him company while he wrote. And he got another raven, which he also named Grip. Mamie described Grip II as "mischievous and impudent." Perhaps that bird was a leg-biter as well.

Grip II was followed by Grip III. Henry Dickens, another of Charles's ten children, said that this raven was so bold that it bullied their mastiff, Turk. The bird would stride up to the large dog's bowl, and Turk would back off as Grip ate the best bits of food. The raven could also crack windowpanes with its beak, and swallow keys, then spit them back up, much to Dickens's amusement.

Because he was so popular, the author received an invitation to visit America and talk about his books. His wife, Catherine, came along, but she was worried about leaving the children. To comfort her on the long journey, Charles Dickens's friend Daniel Maclise painted a picture of Charley, Katey, Mamie, and the new baby, Walter. He put Grip II in the painting as well. Catherine gave the picture a special place in every hotel room where she and Charles stayed.

Before they got to Philadelphia, Dickens got a note from an American writer who wanted to meet him. The man had read *Barnaby Rudge* and liked it. He was amused by the raven. He'd even written a good review in the *Saturday Evening Post*, a highly respected newspaper—though in it he said that it would have been an even *better* book if the raven had croaked throughout to foretell doom.

The American writer was not famous . . . yet. His name was Edgar Allan Poe, and he was rather poor. He was having a hard time trying to support himself and his wife by writing mysteries and horror stories.

He showed up at Dickens's hotel room in a plain suit and mended gloves. Charles Dickens greeted him in a velvet vest with a gold chain and a green necktie with a diamond clasp. Poe most likely noticed the painting of Grip and the Dickens children. He was delighted to discover that the bird in *Barnaby Rudge* was based on Dickens's own pet.

The two men talked about books and poems. Dickens promised to try and get Poe's work published in Great Britain. (He did not succeed.) Poe's stories were published in many popular American magazines, but he still wasn't famous.

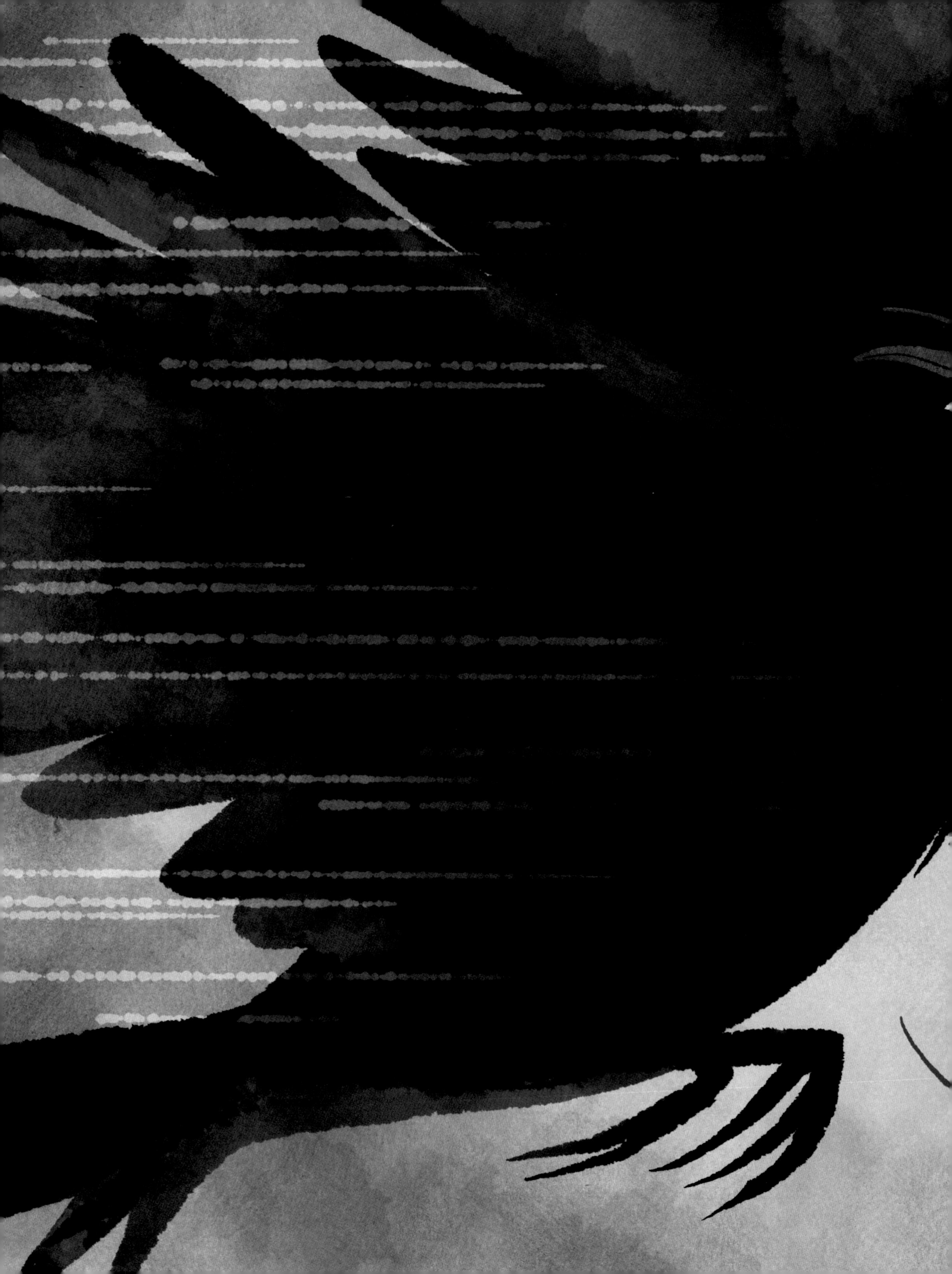

He needed a hit. And, according to most Poe scholars, Grip the raven provided it. Several years after meeting Dickens, Poe put the bird into a spooky poem called "The Raven." In the poem, a raven mysteriously appears and reminds the narrator of his lost love, which drives the man insane. But this bird is not a big talker. Throughout the poem, it croaks just one word:

"Nevermore."

"The Raven" was published in 1845 in the *New York Evening Mirror*, a weekly newspaper that covered arts and literature as well as the local news. It was an instant success, and it made Edgar Allan Poe a celebrity. He was recognized everywhere.

Children would follow him in the street, flapping and croaking until the poet would spin around and say:

"Nevermore."

Then the children would run off, squealing. Yet for all his newfound fame, Poe was still poor. The poem earned him hardly any money at all, though it became and still remains one of the best-known poems in the world.

Charles Dickens outlived Poe and wrote more renowned books, including his most beloved work, *A Christmas Carol*. The painting of his children and Grip II hangs in the Charles Dickens Museum—the London house where he once lived. Next to the picture is a stuffed raven in a glass case. But it isn't Grip. It is a bird that was owned by Bransby Williams, an actor who often performed scenes from Dickens's books on stage. So where is Charles Dickens's raven?

After Dickens died, Grip was bought by a gentleman who would later become the mayor of London. Then the bird passed from one collector to another until at last she was purchased by Colonel Richard Gimbel, a pilot, professor, and department store founder, who had a treasury of rare books, particularly ones by Charles Dickens and Edgar Allan Poe. Gimbel was from Philadelphia, the city where Dickens and Poe had met. In his will, he left his entire collection of Poe's work to the Philadelphia Free Library. Along with that, he donated Grip.

Today, anyone who visits the library can see the raven who inspired two of the world's best known authors. If you close your eyes, you can picture her chasing Charley, Katey, and Mamie around the room and biting ankles, while their famous father dreamed up his next book. And you can imagine another group of children, flapping and croaking behind a poor and talented poet, then scattering like a flock of birds when he whirled around and spoke the magic word:

"Nevermore."

More Grip(p)s

The Tower of London has been a fortress, a palace, a prison, and a treasury. It houses the Crown Jewels, and it once featured a menagerie of exotic animals, most of which eventually went to the London Zoo. Today the Tower's most famous animals are its ravens. Several of them have been named for Charles Dickens's Grip—except their names are spelled *Gripp*.

There is a legend that there must always be at least six ravens at the Tower, or else the Tower and the kingdom will fall. During World War II, the Tower was bombed. Gripp and his mate, Mabel, were the only survivors. Prime Minister Winston Churchill ordered more ravens to be brought to the Tower—and so the kingdom was saved!

Today, there is another Gripp at the Tower of London. Like all of the other ravens there, his wings are trimmed so that he can't fly far away. He doesn't say "Nevermore" nor any other words, but he is as clever as all ravens are. You can take a tour of the Tower and see Gripp and the other ravens, but don't feed or annoy them—like Charles Dickens's Grip, all of the Tower ravens can bite!

The Smartest Birds

Ravens are members of the *corvid*—crow—family. Corvids and parrots are considered to be the most intelligent of all birds. In fact, corvids may well be as smart as apes. They will make and use tools and solve puzzles to get food. They are known to use objects as toys and to play. A popular video shows a raven using a plastic lid as a sled to slide down a roof.

This author had an amazing experience with a raven at the London Zoo. She was wearing a poncho that had pompoms on it. The zoo's raven stuck its beak through the bars of its cage and pulled off a pompom. The bird tossed it back and forth to its mate. Then, when it got tired of the game, it returned the pompom to me—right in the palm of my hand!

Can ravens talk? Yes, but in general only the birds in captivity will imitate human speech. They can also imitate many other sounds and beings. In the wild, they have been known to mimic wolves and foxes to get these canids to break open carcasses so that the ravens may feed.

Are they evil? Despite legends and the ominous bird in Edgar Allan Poe's poem, ravens are no more evil than any predators. They do kill other animals—and sometimes other ravens. But they can show kindness and empathy to each other and to humans. Charles Dickens knew their good and bad sides—and that's why he was able to write about ravens so very well.

Selected Bibliography/Webography

Avesnoir.com/charles-dickens-grip-the-raven/

BBC.com/culture/story/20150820-the-mysterious-tale-of-charles-dickenss-raven

BBC.com/news/uk-england-london-48308322

Britishportraits.org.uk/blog/doting-parents-maclise-portrait-of-the-dickens-children
-and-grip-by-louisa-price/

Charlesdickenspage.com/dickens-and-poe.html

Freelibrary.org/blog/post/3554

Lithub.com/meet-the-beloved-pet-ravens-of-charles-dickens/

London-overlooked.com/dickens-raven/

Mentalfloss.com/article/70095/9-mournful-facts-about-edgar-allan-poes-raven

Openculture.com/2016/10/charles-dickens-edgar-allan-poe-met.html

Poetryfoundation.org/poems/48860/the-raven

Skaife, Christopher, *The Ravenmaster: My Life with the Ravens at the
Tower of London*, New York: Farrar, Straus and Giroux, 2018.

Thevintagenews.com/2018/11/02/raven/

Watson, Nicola J., *The Author's Effects: On Writer's House Museums*,
Oxford, UK: Oxford University Press, 2020.